One Stone

One Stone

Barbara Pelman

Ekstasis Editions

(Wilson)
love to Sheri-D —
with thanks for your
support &
encouragement,
and looking
forward to
time together
in poetry —
love, Barbara
June 2005

Library and Archives Canada Cataloguing in Publication

Pelman, Barbara
     One stone / Barbara Pelman.

Poems.
ISBN 1-894800-37-0

     I. Title.

PS8631.E464O53 2005   C811'.6   C2005-907097-5

Published in 2005 by:
Ekstasis Editions Canada Ltd.   Ekstasis Editions
Box 8474, Main Postal Outlet   Box 571
Victoria, B.C. V8W 3S1   Banff, Alberta T0L 0C0

THE CANADA COUNCIL | LE CONSEIL DES ARTS
FOR THE ARTS | DU CANADA
SINCE 1957 | DEPUIS 1957

BRITISH
COLUMBIA
ARTS COUNCIL
Supported by the Province of British Columbia

One Stone has been published with the assistance of grants from the Canada
Council for the Arts and the British Columbia Arts Council administered by
the Cultural Services Branch of British Columbia.

to my daughter, Lara

and to my parents, Sol and Minnie Pelman

Contents

STONE

Stone in the river
that turns
in the drift of tide
stone from mountain
stone from the fiery centre
earth stone, water stone,
wearing to sliver
of light, quartz stone,
stone sharp
and angled, knife stone

hone me down
to the edge of light
stone to sand to glass
in a desert wind
sirocco blowing over hot
stone, stone that blinds,
bruises the body

breathe the hot wind
stone over desert
bury the city in a stone
cavern, bury the echoes —
sirocco keening — in the stone

breaking, its edges
rainbows, stone
melting, veins, arteries,
rivers of stone

Broken Stone

After Winter

The voice of the last cricket
across the first frost
is one kind of goodbye:
So thin a sliver of singing
                    Carl Sandburg

The air feels starched and freshly ironed
no wrinkles in a flat blue sky.
My fingers are cold as I bury daffodil bulbs
hopefully, for spring —
cut the rosebush, the last red rose
            brittle and paper-thin.
Oregon juncos
startle the pine, disappear into hawthorn tree.
At my ear,
the voice of the last cricket

clicks into the twilight
accordion pleats of sound and silence.
The daylight shrinks
into evening —
dark attends my going out
            and my coming home
The maple tree is now
            calligraphy in a winter language.
Leaves break into icy pieces
across the first frost.

Another winter
I count the losses:
a house on the water
summers adrift in a wood boat
evenings in the cockpit wrapped in blankets
three stockings on the mantel
my name warm in his mouth —
his name now whittled to an initial.
Our photographs in a storage locker
is one kind of goodbye.

I fold my words
into smoothly ironed piles of winter and summer:
rosehip. freesia. snowberry,
meadow lark. swoop of swallow.
I gather pens, Chinese brush,
India ink, charcoal —
cup the darkness in my hand like a flame
blow breath through a silver flute
in D minor —
so thin a sliver of singing.

Journey

The Lord said to Abram, "Go forth from your native land
and from your father's house to the land that I will show you."
                                    Genesis 12.1

You must leave your home —
the one you built from its green roots,
the windows where you watched light rise
across the hills, the tide disrobe the beach,
starfish purple the shore.

Give away the Haida masks, the painting
on the wall beside your bed, the pillow
you've embroidered, the stone turtle
you bought together as a gift.

You will be shown the way —
in books with awkward titles, dream hieroglyphics,
small stones thrown in the sand,
dull coins and dry sticks;
learn the text of ancient sorrows.

If you listen hard
you might hear the language
you buried — with your paints and brushes,
your bold body, your song.

Your hand on the latch,
sun setting on the stained glass windows,
never mind the goodbyes.
Close the door and go.

Hunger

I've come back to the country where I was happy
changed. Passion puts no terrible strain on me now
I wonder what will take the place of desire.
                              Linda Gregg

1.   She learns to eat the world
        with her eyes. The precision of holes
        around a single tree
        watching woodpeckers
        flash red through the green

2.   She memorizes the names of lichen and moss —
        taste these words:
        Ribbed Bog, Forking Bone, Questionable Rock-Frog
        Lanky
                Step
                        Twisted Ulota

3.   She wears her heavy socks to bed
        hunches over the blankets, nose and pen to paper:
                poems at midnight

4.   She listens to stories of lovers
                in Amsterdam
        holding hands across handlebars
                in Japan
        skin reaching for skin
                in Portugal
        She cannot return to countries
                empty of him.

5.   She knows:
            to be without desire
            is to be contained.

6.   Not the empty glass —
        not the bowl held up for rice —

                the bowl turned over
                the hand across the top of the wine glass

        Thank you
                I have enough.
                        I want to be hungry.

Reginald Hill Road

a suite of sonnets

BUILDING THE HOUSE

We watched the bulldozers scoop a path of green,
once, salal and blackberry, now a hole
and now a staircase, chimney, now the walls.
We drank our coffee balanced on the boards

that soon would be a terracotta floor
ready for dancing, looked out at empty windows
that would fill with cedar and arbutus
branches curved and bending to the water.

Soon the Aga stove, its ponderous warmth
tucked into a corner, a counter to lean
our elbows as we talked and baked the morning
muffins, or stirred a curry, simmered the soup.

A house to curl itself around our skin —
or so we dreamed — and let the debts close in.

RED TILES

When the floor was laid in the great room, the red tiles
gleaming and the windows dark with the shadow of cedar,
walls still sharp with paint and the smell of linseed,
before the couches and tables arrived, we danced —

offered our favorite music to each other:
klezmer rhythms from my childhood, fado
guitar, its dark Portuguese lament;
African chants and heartbeat drums, a thumb

piano and Caribbean socca
songs for a carefree life we never had:
ferry rides to work at six a.m.,
tired eyes stuck to computer screens

at midnight. Long days and nights apart
talks that never had a chance to start.

BATHTUB

Saturday mornings we'd linger in the bath
surrounded by tiles we'd bought in Portugal:
he chose the pattern, while I smiled and thought
the green and earthy tones seemed rather bland.

I would have chosen the blue and yellow birds
we saw on walls and narrow corridors
in Albuferia, where fado music
wound a lament through cobbled alleyways.

A bathtub built for two, in a corner
where windows overlooked the trees, green
and blue echoed the sky and water; we held
our tentative marriage in this pleasant frieze.

We washed each other, talked as water cooled
and passions trickled elsewhere, elsewhere fuelled.

AGA

Owning an Aga is more than just owning a range, it's living a way of life. It's a love affair that only Aga customers could express.
    Aga Magazine

A stove that costs as much as a car? my daughter
said. You must be kidding. You don't even like
to cook. Why don't you take a trip, buy
a motorcycle, dye your hair purple?

But we wanted a cooker, the Rolls Royce
of kitchens, four ovens, a thousand pounds
of British racing green luxury, a stove
that would roast a pheasant to perfection.

Mornings he'd lean against the Aga's warmth
with cups of coffee, and I'd lean against
him, his beard a sandpaper kiss
his arms a comfort I'd hate to leave.

Like a wise green Buddha, looking on,
knowing all the answers, offered none.

LAUNDRY ROOM

He wanted to place the laundry room in the basement.
It's too noisy for upstairs — he said.
Though the hotel laundry rooms in Bangkok,
Jakarta, Jordan saw more of his socks
and underwear than I ever did.
So the machines rattled and coughed in a room
whose unfinished walls reminded us
of bills not paid, a mortgage to make us wince.

Walls still penciled with measurements, walls
with studs like hungry ribs, the builder packing
his angry tools, before he finished plans
for a hot tub on the wooden deck, trees
and shrubs and deerproof flowers, curving steps—
a blueprint of opulence unchecked.

BASEMENT

Mornings I'd peek around the basement door
anticipating the first round glimpse of tail
like a severed earthworm on the stairs —
and under the guillotine, a clump of grey.

At first I dumped the mouse — still tightly trapped —
into a paper bag and into the bay,
watched it carefully as it bobbed and sank
prayed the crabs would cough up the wire springs.

It left its droppings, like bits of wild rice,
leftovers from a forgotten gourmet meal
in old newspaper, boxes from our past:
discarded wedding gifts, used books, debris.

Like our shattered future lying ahead
the basement was a long held breath of dread.

Ending Up Where We Are

after Galway Kinnell

Here, at my back, I feel his foot prodding me out of bed, the windows
       still black, the floor still cold: 5:30 am
Here, the bathroom tiles warm my bare feet — our fancy Roman
       touch —and my feet are grateful —
Here, he leans against the AGA stove, coffee mug in hand, another
       stretched to me, milk steaming, and I lean against his terry
       bathrobe my cheek against his beard
Here, I turn on the ignition, shattering the silence of wind and
       water, guiding the car backwards up the dark driveway
Here I split the darkness with my headlights, cedar with stars
       on its arms, tall firs, arbutus curling heavily down the bank
Here I remember the warmth of the bed, the uncertainty of his back
Here I wait in the ferry line, behind Mark on his motorcycle,
       Paul in his pickup, Larry ready to throw some jokes
       about teachers' easy lives:
Do you see me, Larry? Here I spread my snowfall of papers
       across the dashboard, nose to grindstone, pen to paper
Here I watch the sun rise over the Coast Mountains,
       yellow halo around blue islands, and wonder, but only
       for a moment, what am I doing and why am I doing it
       and am I the person I thought I was going to be
       that day I watched the ring claim my finger
Here I smooth the car down the Pat Bay highway, trees
       and houses gather outline, shape colour as the sun
       slides up the sky
Here I wonder where, and how, and why, we end up where we are

Here a plane skrills above the highway, its wheels down,
     like an osprey, fishing
Here the Elk Lake station advertises gas cheaper than the full tank
     I pumped yesterday
Here I decide that contentment is worth its price and wasn't I content?
Here the quartet of Mozart's Requiem weaves soprano into alto,
     bass into tenor, and I slide into my parking spot, turn off
     the motor, sit, listen, smooth one more moment into a
     tallis of praise
Here, almost too late, I wonder what I am going to do today
     with thirty sneakered and distracted teenagers who are
     perhaps wondering what excuse they will use today and
     whether Tracy really meant what she said and whether
     Kent will notice her new hairstyle and if there are
     the right shoes for grad anywhere on the face of the earth
Here I notice, definitely too late, that one sock is black
     and the other navy.
Here I wonder, but only for a moment, what I might be doing
     with three extra hours a day spent not treadmilling up and
     down the highway on and off the ferry — maybe watch the
     woodpecker drill the balsam tree plant daffodil bulbs, and
     tulips for the deer, walk country roads, dip bare toes over
     the edge of the wharf

     but only for a moment.

Letter to Pygmalion

What did he think —
that I would follow his command
when the marble melted
and I become flesh?

That I would lie still
smiling, smiling —
his creation?

This jade necklace
like a soft chain around my neck;
these gold anklets,
silver headdress:
nails riveted to my skull.

Let me love you,
he croons,
all I ask is your devotion

I will protect you
cherish you;
all I ask are your eyes
your lips
your soul.

All you need to do:
Relax. Lie still. Smile.

I left the note on the table
hitched a ride to the harbour
set sail on the first tide.

Birdsong

Another thrush, its white underbelly
like a small shout. And at my feet,
pale lavender, a throat of yellow,
crocus — whose song is spring:
I am always here
under darkness.

I look up to a watercolour sky
the sun heavy on my winter coat
earth squelching with yesterday's rain,
clouds thin and meandering and far away
above the darker blue of the Olympics —
white feathers of last month's snow.

Gray branches flaked with old skin —
at the edge of the long bones, a soft trembling
Slash of silence, then sound
a fever of calling: I am here.
Where are you.

Sestina for a Solo Dance

How little I could say
to him, who should have been the one
I could say anything to, whose hands
would cradle my words like a mother
and I could sing, could dance —
lay my burden down.

But he let me down.
There was nothing I could say
into his silence, that danced
in circles away from me, leaving only one
on stage, speechless (like no mother
I know). In his hands

I was putty, and his hands
shaped me, smoothed me down
to a smiling flatness. My mother
told me later, "I was afraid to say
anything." Now I am the one
to tap out the circular dance

on a singular dance
floor. Clap hands
Everyone!
Watch me tear down
the banners that say
Not. Never. No. I will mother

the growing self, become my own mother,
learn new steps to an old dance —
a one-legged polka, a limping tango. I'll say
the words I never said, with my hands
flying, placing each syllable down
in choreography —one by one.

The stage is set again. One
lone flute plays a mother's
lullaby of loss and comfort. Count the measure down:
let the dance
begin, step by halting step, hands
holding air, say

Yes. One more time, yes. I will learn this solo dance
my mother never taught me, with hands
open, all barriers down: this is what I have to say.

Demon Lover

He sews himself inside
her skin. Wherever she goes he
is with her;
when she breathes he
sips on the dark side of her nipples
and loops his tongue around
each aureole.

When she talks, he murmurs kisses
along the muscles of her throat
and her words become sweet and crust over
like old candy.

His dark eyes
surround her hazel ones
and she sees the world through his, blanched
and hard-lined:
nothing of the soft edges
and chiaroscuro she sees
in her dreams —
where he cannot go.

All day he licks at her blood
holds her tendons in his tongue, curls
along the whorls of her ear.
When she picks up the pen
his fingers slide along the paper:
nice, now, he says, make it nice.
Say pretty words, don't tell
our secrets.

How will she separate?
Turn herself inside out,
until he is merely a coat
she can take off.

This will take time:
a comb to scrape her skin
wind to blow through her veins,
a river to cleanse her blood —

morning light
to chant her name.

I Will Arise and Go Now

after W.B. Yeats, "Lake Isle of Innisfree"

I

And when there is no Innisfree,
no bee-loud glade or anything more
than a townhouse crowded with things
none of them growing or green:
when the gray pavements pound like
jack hammer through cement,
and the linnet's wings whisper
a feeble song, when
crickets are crushed under booted
feet in a hurry to get anywhere —

What will be heard
in the deep heart's core?

II

Saltspring Island: the patio
overlooking sun on morning water:
nerves and tendons tuned to the woodpecker's
drumming on balsam, or the owl's
last call across the harbour.
The yellow flash of evening grosbeak,
the blue call of kingfisher and the dark
hood of Oregon junco —now merely blurred
memories on retina. The house sold,
documents signed and filed away.

III

Losses make small things
valuable. Even in the city, a crow dips
precarious feathers into a birdbath
on a small quilt of green; thyme and lavender
patch a window box. My neighbor cuts
the blackberry snarls but I coax them
into my welcoming bowl: one wayward
tomato plant in a clay planter
survives a winter, grows
a garden.

One Leaf

Ah, heart, I cannot scorn the armies of your pain.
It is night, air, and I am drunk again on words,
One stone would be enough,
one leaf, a feast.

> Patrick Lane, "How the Heart Stinks with its Devotions"

Paint on a scarlet smile,
happiness the best revenge, they say:
laugh and dance, put grief in the closet,
lock the doors, mail the key to Siberia.
It is better, they say, you'll thank him one day.
Listen to the old platitudes: rainbows follow rain;
where you stumble, there is treasure:
suffering builds character — all the noise
chuffed like a dreary mantra, again and again —
ah heart, I cannot scorn the armies of your pain

its regrets, every one knife-keen,
the dead armies of memory, stinking in mud,
planes overhead parachuting enemies
into the life I build with twigs and pebbles.
Each stone dredged from the river,
hauled in a basket of thin reed; windows curve
around a breath of silence. I carve letters
with the edge of a sword: fireflies,
pyractomena borealis— like bright birds.
It is night, air, and I am drunk again on words

place them on my tongue like a wafer, sip
them like sacrament, line them up like soldiers
risen again, collect them in boxes,
trunks, houses, mountains-
use them as a rock to build upon:
feel the rough
texture, precarious alphabet
of earth and fire —
if words could build a world, like love
one stone would be enough

In this desert of beauty, this firefly land
where words name each bird, each flower,
tongue sliding down bark,
club moss a cloud of green on the palate —
I build a small cabin in a green oasis,
skin of cedar, leaves that weave
a rooftop. I set on the pine table
one white stone, one yellow rose,
one bowl of mountain water, place
one leaf, a feast.

Writing a Sestina

Choose the words wisely or you'll hate
them by the end of thirty nine lines.
Perhaps a story will work best —
a rambling narrative that lounges
against an image and takes its shoes
off, waltzes in the meadow of a refrain.

Better write all the words like a vertical refrain
along the edges of the page, or you'll hate
the mess you make, have to take off your shoes
roll up your sleeves along with the wretched lines.
Maybe it's time to slide into the chaise lounge
consider the career of a plumber as a best

option. Though it's best
to keep moving, think of Anne Lamott's refrain
about the shitty first draft. Lounging
will get you nowhere, and you'll hate
yourself for giving up. Keep your eyes on the line
plod onwards, trade your dancing shoes

for work boots, and remember the closet of shoes
you'll buy when this damn sestina wears its best
tuxedo to the ball. There's a long line
of quitters in Dante's Inferno, the echoing refrain
"Abandon hope", a hate-
ful melody, buried deep in that beckoning lounge

chair. Don't go there. You can lounge
later, skip and flutter shoeless
in the open meadows of free verse, that you once hated —
After this ordeal, free verse is the brightest of the best.
Only one more stanza, then the refrain —
the envoy, three little lines

and then it's done. Hang this sestina on a long line
and go fishing. Read a book, fill a bath you can lounge
in, nibble on almond croissants and sing a joyful refrain:
No more sestinas! Throw your shoes
in the air, the best
is yet to come — only one more hated

stanza. Time to drag out the fishing line, take off the toe-scrunching shoes,
Sestinas are not the best poems for lounging in,
An endless refrain of reckless words, ones you knew you'd hate.

Leiomyoma

You had a rare benign tumor, the doctor says.
You do not have cancer,
The kidney we took out
                    wasn't malignant.
Aren't you thrilled?

My fingers wander along the 10 inch incision
a slightly raised ridge of skin and muscle.
I should have been vacationing in London right now—
I could have been in the Cancer Clinic right now.

One day, not today
            I will put my affairs in order
One day, not today
            I will regret the dancing I never did
            the villa on the Greek island I never located
            the flute limp in its velvet case
            the bicycle rusting on the patio
            the country paths not taken, the villages beyond the hill.

The days will march towards a wall of dread
            the distance deepening
                        between lilies and crickets
                        the warm breath on a soft cheek
                        head on a familiar shoulder
                        the moment when eye meets eye
                        and love happens

Not today.

No Longer in Service

1

The bonsai quince pushes out a small pink blossom
wilts in a day or two

leaves huddled on the bare branches
already dead before they fall

Somewhere in this body
under this skin
between these ribs

a heart is counting out its last measures

2

The little deaths that have already happened —
places I no longer live
Haida masks which once stared from familiar walls
friends who no longer mention my name
        remember my voice

There is a woman now —
        blonde, smooth skinned
        sleeps where I slept:
        her back stretches toward him
        her hands circle him as mine did,

        His voice lingers on her name in the early morning

The accident which brought them together
        killed us
I live on the other side of that death
look out on a Sunday morning to a view of a new world:
south to the Olympic peninsula
across city rooftops

I left a skin behind
and live now
        in one a little more wrinkled and weary

3

The truck slid on black ice
     tumbled down a steep bank
     into a channel of the Thompson river

     While I was buying Christmas presents at home,
     He reached down to the passenger seat
     the wrecked Pathfinder
          where she crouched
          the water circling her ankles.
     He gave her his hand:
     nobody was hurt.

     Accidental death
     of a marriage

4

If he had said to me
       "I'll love you for twenty years
       then I'll leave"
Would I have said yes?
Taken my chances?
Looked elsewhere?

If they told us
       "You have sixty years
       then your heart, lungs, brain
       will stop"
Would we take our chances
figure sixty years is good enough?
       Hope for a miracle?

5

My mother wants her children to choose
some of her Royal Albert tea-cups
her gold-trimmed plates and mismatched glasses,
pearl earrings and silver cuff links:
    "so you won't fight over them after I'm gone"

The opal ring my father gave her for their fiftieth anniversary:
How will I wear
    that long-lasting love
    around my bare finger?

6

All that has been gathered
will be dispersed:
four file cabinets of lesson plans
        in a school dumpster
books with well-loved words
        scattered into libraries and used bookstores
Someone will open the cover page
        read: B. P. 653-4823

A number no longer in service

foundation

Biography

As a child, she was a dancer, lifted
hand to wooden *barre*
a long line of happiness from outstretched arm
to outstretched leg:
a perfect *arabesque*

In her twenties, she slept on yellow sheets
gave her house key to lovers:
a boy with green eyes,
another who taught her
the shape of birds in air

One lover left her a winter daughter

The one she married
gave her a house on the water,
twenty years:
a kind of forever.

Now, she makes her dancing slippers
out of paper and ink
folds *plies* into metaphor,
bends sound around a *pirouette*
through the ochres and umbers
of her thoughts—
her *entrechats* slide
across a silent stage.

Mapping the Wind

This year the hurt is not so deep. The days
that stretch along a wild and high plateau
between ravines of grief—that carve the cheeks
and tear the lungs—grow longer, ebb and flow.
A scholar of sorrow, I wrap myself in words,
name the chasms and the hills, chart
the murderous and the mild winds: *sirocco*
the sighing wind; *sumatra*, the raging heart
that blasts the growing bud; *borasco*
the bitter wind that sucks the morning dew
and leaves the soul a desert. Now I know
that gentle *tramontana* soon will bring
the spirit wind, that blows from somewhere near
where squalls are tamed, and I'll learn again to sing.

At the Edge of the Photograph

My mother's green satin dress
sheens even in black and white,
in the middle of the family
photograph. A wave of hair dips
over one eye. Her two youngest
lean toward her, nestle
in her skirts, press their small bodies
against her cool sleeves. My father
is absent. Beside her,
how small he looks, my older brother
his hair tightly curled and oiled
a nonchalant smile
on an acne-free face,
tie neatly knotted, hands
calm on his lap. I am
at the edge of the photograph,
skirt stiff in black and white
velvet, a black bodice hiding breasts
too small to wrinkle the fabric.
If I pull the corners of my mouth
up, nobody will know.
If I move two more steps—
I will be out
of the picture.

The Lady of Shalott

I have seen sunlight nest on the water,
its pale feathers, orange head;
clouds of blue and lavender in a long tail:
sunrise on the ferry to work.

Their colours have walked across my eyes,
onto the paper without a stopover. I do not feel
the gulls' glide, light on dark: just words
plugging the empty places, painting
the white-washed walls. I have seen

trees drummed with snow, a sky blasting blue
like a trumpet. I write it down.
Turn away from the thrill of deliquescent sun
against indigo hills, gaze without desire
the monarch lifting its tiger wings.

Easy to close the door, watch the shift
of light against a mirror, rainbows
in the bevelled edges. I sketch the sparrow
springing in the holly — through a window
closed against the winter storm, the summer
breeze — autumn humming
of death, spring singing of stubborn
beginnings.

Bless This Day

after e.e. cummings

If I could thank, if I could bless this amazing
day, a clean spanking sky and everything
sparkle and laugh, just being alive, the yes
of a morning grin — but I cannot except
in shadow smile, though the earth breaks out
of its cage at dawn and its wings glide
on the yellow sun opening inevitable horizons
yet seeing not feeling   touching not tingling
not any — all no   all maybe   all when   all
perhaps — and still doubt the sky blue out-
stretched along crimson and indigo, cloud fingers
on a D major chord, singing hallelujah
for the beauty of it all — how can eyes
open, heart hear?

Woman With Hat and Coffee

after Edward Hopper's painting, "Automat"

Here I'll wrap myself in a dark night
and a cup of coffee. My hat will hide my shame —
Stranded. Dumped. Played a little game
with me the loser. Down without a fight.
I should have known he'd take me for a ride —
those lovely lips. Those lies. That enchanting smile —
Let's run away to Nice, he said. The miles
between us and our lousy past; the tide
will wash away our guilt, will cleanse the pain.
Just you and me, he said. And now it's me —
no turning back, the letter cut the ties
and so it's done. In this dark place I'm free.
What freedom means is darkness, and the rain
which grows the hidden bud of self again.

Two Poems For My Grandmother

I. NAMESAKE

They gave me your name
and my aunts curled it around their tongue:
Basha Fega, they smiled,
smoothing my hair with their fingers.

Lovers, my fingers in their rough hair
whispered my secret name in the curve of my throat,
the sound strange on their awkward Protestant tongues.
But I could not hear.

They whispered but I couldn't hear
didn't know who might arise
in answer to their calling.
I knew nothing about you, *Basha Fega*.

Nothing of your garden, your children rooted
in another country, their wives in bright kitchens
in the New World. They left you
or did you wish to stay?

You stayed for the song, perhaps.
Fiddle and clarinet in klezmer beat,
or the taste of twisted bread
baked in a clay oven.

I never learned how to bake bread,
wanted a degree in science, a research lab:
turned from the old ways. What could you teach me,
if I knew your name?

Perhaps you knew—you smiled,
left alone, finally. The bread slowly baking,
the roses musky in their Russian soil.
The pen ready, the instruments tuned.

My pen is ready too; dips and drops a stone
onto the crisp page. The window is open.
I hear your song, sung in an empty room.
In the echoes, I speak your name.

II. She Responds

I stayed in the Old Country. Here there is music
in a heartbeat I can understand. The soil is black
and the roses I sing to speak only Russian.
The air of Grozyanka is a good yeast.

The loaves curl and twist, the yeast rises in a Sabbath blessing.
I lay the linen tablecloth, the silver candlesticks.
Dark clouds and the lark's singing
guide the Sabbath Queen to our home.

We gather, Shloimo with his fiddle and Arye on clarinet.
Sometimes Itzik brings his accordion.
I am the voice that weaves the music:
How can I leave?

When the men leave, I dance, my skirts counterpoint the beat
of hands clapping, my shawl unraveling behind me.
I look at my husband, watching me, and know
tonight will bring another child.

And that child too will leave
raise a family in another country, where there is no music
to wrap around a summer night or warm a winter.
Give one of them to me, give her my name

My grand-daughter, let her hear it, my name
deep in the places she must listen —
where roses sleep, and thorns scrape the light.
My name in the stillness, *Basha Fega*.

Exodus

stories from my great-grandmother

I sit on the wooden steps at the back of the general store—
My husband stands inside at the till
glasses balanced on his thin nose
He smiles at our neighbors
dispenses pickles and advice.

I skip the pickles
Give advice only.
They come to ask me questions,
these villagers, their shawls tight
in clenched fingers, their eyes
searching. I find answers for them
in the books I'm not allowed to read in the synagogue

Never mind, a woman's connection to God is personal.

I watch the world swagger and limp—
the gravel path winds through the village
leading to no place we can go.

I watch the Cossack soldier
a glint in his eye and his boots
nudging pale skin —
my neighbor Hymie's son:
"Get up, Jewboy," he says.

Some things are easier to heal—
the warts on Shloimo's hands
the grief in Hannah's heart
the correct prayer to get a chicken to lay an egg.
I lay my hands on Shlomo's hands
gently rub yellow oil of celandine into his calloused skin,
kiss the tears from Hannah's eyes
turn her in the right direction.

Hymie swears he will leave here,
take his family to America
Soon we will be a village of one —
wailing and chanting to the empty skies
where Hanna's violin cadenzas
whispered and Shlomo sang to the wind.

How They Met

for my parents

She loved him
as only a desolate fourteen-year-old
loves what is unattainable.
She offered her house
to meet with his girlfriends —
her parents absent and neglectful,
their parents strict.
She even offered to call them:
Mona, Esther, Sarah —
all his girls.
Where did she go? Upstairs
to her room? Outside, under
the apple tree? The small red fruit.
I see her, homework on her lap,
wrenching her mind away
from that fierce twosome on the couch.

A few months later, he put his hand
over hers as she dialed a number.
"No", he said, "I came
to see you."
"Took you long enough,"
she said, or should have
if I were writing
her script. Or, "Too late,
I've decided to get
a PhD. All that studying
under the apple tree."
But this is 1930. She
is my mother, daughter
of immigrants.

Instead, she smiled,
thrilled that her patience
bore fruit.

Like all mothers,
offered me the gift
she didn't choose.

They Marry
my parents' anniversary

For seven years,
like Jacob, he worked his way
toward her. Not an ambitious man,
and the times hard, he sold bread,
cut meat, saved his money
and his ardor. A few days
past her 21st birthday, she said,
I can't wait any longer.

I imagine their excitement,
the danger — a marriage ceremony
without a rabbi's blessing.

She chose her dress carefully —
nothing to provoke her mother's
questions, her father's scorn:
a simple print, a hat. Some roses
from the garden, the ring borrowed
from his married sister. He wore
his only suit. It was over
in a minute. They spent the night
in the Hastings Bath House
making steamy love for 25 cents
an hour.

All that summer
they kept their narrow beds
in their parents' houses.
He sold bread,
she typed letters.
They met at the tennis court
gathered an hour into eager hands
wherever they could.

How did her father
find out? What message
in their eyes, the hands that sought
each other. This time
they married under a *chupah*,
her father's reluctant blessing.
They vowed forever.

Their children, grandchildren,
great grandchildren learn
forever from their eyes:
sixty-seven years later.

Nine Days Before Tisha B'Av

Shadow is the place
that interests me.
Under these dark wings
I hide my stubborn bones.
          Kate Braid, "Poem #82, Inward to the Bones"

It is the month of Av —
Nine days before Tisha B'Av,
the destruction of the Temple —
time to shadow our joy
though the sun shines hot
and the sea is fresh and bracing.
While mornings are crisp with possibility
we must remember
the Tower burning, the dark blaze.
Shadow is the place

where hope stumbles
in the rubble of shattered houses:
Baghdad. Ramallah. Tel Aviv —
a child's severed hand grasps the metal seat
of a bombed out school bus in Jerusalem, the City of Peace.
And an oil sheik
or a Manhattan executive
tosses the cost of a country's education
on an office party. It is the gap between loss and greed
that interests me.

In these long summer days
I hold flowers captive
in bright containers, help my daughter
pack for Japan, push a black pen
across a white page, walk the narrow
corridor between couch and computer, think
and ponder and scour the cartons of memory
again and again.
Wonder what strange and unearthly things
under these dark wings

mangle my flight? The fears that freeze
the feathers, shackle the mind:
an empty bed, a body
no longer supple, a table for one.
Turn away from dark, they tell me;
Trust in the hollow bones
of wings, emptiness at the heart
of flight; the zero before counting begins.
But under ribs heavy with the wind's groans
I hide my stubborn bones

She Complains to Moses

You tell me this is better —
this tent in the desert,
the flies
            the wind —
a spirit wind, *Ruach*.
like the dove with hope in her beak
we're free.

Free to starve, I say —
to grieve our losses.

There were some pleasures —
a kind word from the Egyptian guards,
gossiping with friends,
the Sabbath candles.
I woke at dawn
            returned at sunset
did what I had to do.
Whether from fear
            or for love
what does it matter?

You give us a coat of air
call it freedom —
I call it holes and empty space.
I feel the cold,
smell the scent of unknown spices
on limitless horizons
            too far away

How can I fly
with these drooping feathers
            these shuddering wings?

Moujik*

My boots are beginning to feel
        the crushed gravel of the path.
They do not protect me.
The winter wind is cold
and the fireplace
does not warm the corners of the room.

Will the soup bone
        last another day?
Perhaps tomorrow
        the chickens will lay eggs.
Perhaps I will trade the goat for grain.

Let the candles last one more night
and we can welcome in
        the Sabbath.

* *a Russian peasant*

Two Sarahs

SARAI, 3000 B.C.

My feet drag through centuries of desert
follow Abram's straight back-
and that's where I want to go: back.

He had come running in from the fields one day
Honey I have this great idea, he'd said.
Let's leave our home, all our friends,
family, the familiar roads —
sell the furniture and that tapestry
you made. We'll go south, to a place
I don't know yet.

Why? I said.

But it was no use. He was called, he said.
So I packed dishes, clothing, the tapestry,
loaded them onto the mules and the backs
of our servants.
Lot came too, and his family —
they thought it was a great adventure.
My friend Hannah waved goodbye
ran after us to press her best linen tablecloth
into my arms.
My eyes stretched back to the land:

To the olive tree I sat under
when I learned I was barren. To the blacksmith
who was teaching me to make bracelets.
To the river where
God and I spoke softly in stone words.

SARAH, 1915

When we went to America, landed at Ellis Island,
they changed our name, said it was
unpronounceable. Hymie said,
Who cares? We're new people now!
But there were no jobs for new people here
in America.

So Hymie plays cards, sings in the choir,
dreams of riches.
I smooth the white tablecloth my mother gave me
before I left, place the candles in the silver candlesticks
from our house in Minsk. Gubernia.
Go in peace, she'd said.

At the Sabbath table
refugees, our boarders, talk
of the Old Country, their long faces
and long stories.
I bought another house with the rent money,
and from the liquor we smuggled
past the border. I push the buggy
clanking of rum, holding Sammy's small hand,
Norman sleeping under the blankets,
over the bottles: *Shabbas* wine, Russian vodka, gin.

Perhaps God is a drunkard
in America.

In It Again

Morning. Drag
sleep from my bones, creak
to the shower, fumble
with faucets, each step longing
to return to bed.
But the day must begin, and I
in it.

What alternatives?
A headstone
on a forgotten hill, my name
crossed out of phone books, an estate sale
of unmarked boxes.

In the mirror:
dark eyes, energetic
curls, skin in need
of ironing.

On the breakfast table:
a porcelain plate
linen napkin.
The coffeemaker half-filled.

I open the front door
let the day unravel
a long scarf of details
to a small knot;
tuck simplicity
into a back pocket
for lunch.

Resplendant Like a God

after Pablo Neruda

In the bare corridor
I hear the petals
float
around my feet.
They gather in large clouds.
The room beside me
looks out to the sea —
the hills,
the sky
all slide into a spume of green.
How like flowers
to cleave into one
blaze of light,
resplendent like a god.
They are
companions, rich
and empty, they lift me.
My lover, visible
in the corridor,
        Cleanse me.

Palindrome to a Married Man

You want me:
another pleasure to be grabbed
on the long rush to the grave
a memory to tuck away
while your wife reads in bed
while your daughter helps you in the garden.
Seize the day, you say.
I am not on the shelf
for your borrowing
I'm not on loan
I am not a well you can fill
a hole you can dig
a town to be pillaged.
You are
more than I need
less than I want.

Less than I want
more than I need
you are
a town to be pillaged
a hole you can dig.
I am not a well you can fill
I'm not on loan
for your borrowing
I am not on the shelf.
Seize the day, you say
while your daughter helps you in the garden
while your wife reads in bed
a memory to tuck away
on the long rush to the grave
another pleasure to be grabbed —
You want me

Sestina With Roses

At six o'clock the leaves are still bright —
It's a long time between twilight and sunset, a better
light, soft around the edges, the blues deep
as canyons, shifting slurs of yellow, like the roses
you once laid on my doorstep.
I can still see the long box, the green paper, imagine

new roses in the Moorcroft vase you took, imagine
your feet in slippers beside her pink chenille bed, bright
with miracles. I no longer remember your voice, my doorstep
is a threshold to silence, a better
music than the words which dropped like dead roses
in my empty lap. Four years today. A chasm deep

as mystery separates us. Questions deepen
but do not resolve the long spaces. I need to imagine
a new book, me the heroine, my own roses
growing in a back garden, the air rich with scent, bright
saffron and sundusted. Take my pen, write a better
story, arms full of flowers and an open door. Step

forward, lean into the wind of a new world. One door
closes another opens they say. My distrust is deeper
than dread. Even an old discarded book is better
than these white pages. How can I imagine
the end of a line, how to reach its bright
shadows, remove the dead leaves from the roses,

water them with sweat, not tears? Place a rosebush
at the corners of the doorstep,
let each climb like a halo, bright
eglantine, effusion of floribunda, deep
rolling names like Sombreuill, Koricole. Imagine
a garden of my own making — a better

story to tell my grandchildren, surely. A better
air woven of light and shadow, rose-tinted.
Stifle the voices under the chenille bedspread, let the images
pass like clouds, turn away from the doorstep
of others' dreams. Bury the deep
longing in a bright

shroud. The better story is packaged and waiting on the doorstep.
There are no roses in coffined boxes any more. Drink deep
imagine the garden, the long grass, leaves gleaming and bright.

Building a City

Trust

The maple tree still wears the tattered rags
of last summer, reluctant to believe
in emptiness. The garry oak nearby
has no such qualms. He parades bare twisted
branches like bones in an xray, puffs
his buds like warts on arthritic fingers.

In the corner of the garden, the hawthorn
hardly has a moment, between the bright
berries of winter and the white clouds
of blossom in spring, to catch his green
breath. And the dead twigs that were almost
thrown out in November are now
quick and laughing.

Even the maple must admit
the mouths at the end of her dead branches
thrust tongues out,
preparing to sing.

Variations on a Word

Da-da-yenu, Da-da-yenu, Dayenu —
("it would have been enough...")
                    Passover song

It would have been enough
                if I had won the lottery
                        married a rich man
                                for love
                if my hair was thick and blond and shoulder-length
                my eyes, violet
                if I had won the Pulitzer Prize for Poetry

"I've had enough" she said
                He doesn't even know there's anything wrong
                        can't even tell
                                my smile is painted over liquid foundation

                I've had enough of silence
                        of preparing my face
                                for his return

It's never enough
                the small dent
                        in the dessert tray
                all the places to visit:
                        Paris, Prague, Rome,
                        Monserrat, Sagres, Haifa

It is enough
                a small garden, song sparrow
                in the hawthorn tree;
                a long bath with lavender swirls,
                one small stone, cupped in a palm
                thrown like regret into the sea.

Flash the Red Petticoat

It's been three long years. Enough's enough
the grief may fade, as fade it should
The way's been slow, the way's been rough
It's time to get up to no damn good

The grief may fade, and fade it should
Time to bury him up to his neck
It's time to get up to no damn good
Flash the red petticoat, castanets clack

Time to bury him up to his neck
Let the ants crawl out and in
Flash the red petticoat, castanets click
High heels tap and rattle and spin

Let the ants crawl out and in
Nostrils seeping, eyeballs ooze
High heels tap and rattle and spin
Let his skin decay and bruise

Nostrils seeping, eyeballs ooze
Bald head blazing, ears aflame
Let his skin decay and bruise
I'm heading off to a different game

Bald head blazing, ears aflame
The way through death is slow and rough
I'm heading off to a different game
Three long years. Enough's enough.

You're Married

from a line by e.e.cummings

You're married and hands get red washing
dishes washing socks and underwear washing
the thoughts you shouldn't have —
You're married and the couples march two
by two down the aisle, into
the ark. And the waters rise and the
mountains disappear and the earth
is a placid lake and you're married
and your hands are red with blood,
the cut ribbons of dreams splashing on the deck
and you're married and the sun smiles
on all its people and the waters recede
and the sky is red with unwashed
desire and you're married and the sky
is black and your hands are red and
you wash and you wash —

Shattered

And nothing can be sole or whole
That has not been rent.
          William Butler Yeats

1.   Shattered was the word I used
        coming home that night from yoga class.
        "I meant scattered" — I joked
        But twenty years were shattered by these five words:
        "I'm in love with Sarah."

2.   From full to empty in one letter:
        whole
                    hole.

3.   It's the paradox I love
        and dread. Desire is suffering. Love
        what you must lose.
        That damned butterfly.

4.   Half of my life
        on her walls —
        the poet in his garden of pomegranates and rabbits,
        the Chinese acrobats whirling in blues and reds.
        paintings he brought back from China

5.   The closets are finally emptied,
        tweed jackets and silk and wool trousers,
        pressed cotton shirts and one Fraser tie —
        battle dress, he called it,

        the boarding passes he insisted on collecting
        clutter other bowls —
        half the dinnerware
        on another table:
                    set for five.

6.   I'm tired of this.
       Are there no other themes but
       soap opera?
       Rend my clothes, tear out my hair
       stuff the soles of old shoes
            with marriage documents

       Dance on the grave
       in a red dress, bare feet,
       arms open to wind and weather.

7.   Sole self
       in sole possession of.

Doors

She lies on a long sofa,
her eyes shadowed,
a weight of hair like a shutter
across one cheek. She does not
speak, though my words fumble
in the air, a botched pass.
Tell me, I beg her, *tell me*
what to do. She picks
at the silk shawl that drifts
smoothly down her shoulders,
shifts her weight, places
one bare foot on the tiled floor.

See what I'm doing?
she says. *Walk away.*

The scent of her hair —
vanilla, lavender.
The faint slide of silk
on tile, the finality
of doors.

Knees

for Lara

Up from the world
of ankles and heels,
where she ran with dust
bunnies and carpet fringes —
she has balanced herself
on her small feet:
first, rump in the air,
then arms out like gliders.

Master of the Knees of the Universe,
she is eye level
with rhododendron bushes,
early daffodils,
the neighbor's dog.
Companion of
window sills, coffee tables
and sofa seats, she toggles and sprawls
her way
through a lengthening
world.

Her tippling body
stiff legged around bulky
diapers, I follow her,
ready to catch
and comfort. I'm not quick
enough for the fall, the recovery,
the onward slash through space.
She leans over, beheads
a wavering tulip, makes a wide
toppling turn, hands
me her prize.

Shongololo*

Shongololo —
dozens of feet in different directions
not enough brain
to get out of the way.
I pick up one lolling leg
dangle the creature in the humid air —
it twists and wriggles
two thousand toes searching for ground.

Shongololo —
a word in a crisp January classroom
where insects know better than to amble
across a crowded floor
where teenagers in sneakers
larger than a human head
          smash and squish and squelch.

Shongololo —
African lullaby
crooned under mosquito netting:
Watch your feet. Tuck in your toes.
Curl into your mother's
many many arms.

*a millipede, in Zulu

Long Beach With Lara

GETTING THERE

I pick her up along the way —
on Happy Valley Road —
We have only three days
to pack enough to hold us
for two years; enough time left
after the car repairs, visas and passports
have unknitted our time together
down to a thin sleeve.
Ahead is ice-cream,
waterfalls, rocky pools
and lakes like frosted glass
firs and cedars catching sun
in their dark feathers.
The first sense of ocean
is its smell — the sharp green slap
of seaweed, and the high cry of seagulls.
We arrive at a beach curved
into an arm of forest,
waves a quiet heartbeat,
a curl of surf, a scallop of foam —
leaving in its wake the bones of its creatures:
sand dollar, limpet, scallop and clam.

Our room is a narrow strip of beds
under skylight and a dormered roof —
below is a lounge with couches to dream in
a rock fireplace for stormy mornings —
not for this blue and yellow haze of midsummer.

There is time here —
a slow trickle of minutes and moments
time for mother and daughter and
nothing more.

RIDING THE WAVES

At Combers Beach
she heads straight through the surf
arms raised, riding each wave
as it roars to shore.
I follow tenuously, hatted and shirted
camera clicking.
The photos show a smaller
and smaller body, a wider
horizon.
I place hat and shirt and camera
safe from the tide
wander along the shore
finally plunge after her.
She is far away, jumping through green waves
disappearing into white foam
the current taking her
closer to Japan.

MOLLUSC MESSAGES

When the sun hits the beach like that,
we can see lines, curves, shapes and squiggles
written on the shore.
Just under the surface, something hurries
pushing his thick shell through the sand,
weaving around microscopic obstacles —
a rock? a clam? a hermit crab?
From where we stand, it looks like cuneiform,
hieroglyphics — a Sanskrit alphabet
of mollusk monks, carefully meditating
across the centuries.
We have found the husks
of their ancestors, collected them along with
sand dollar skeletons and limpets.
Knuckle sized, in subtle shades
grays and burgundy and teal blue.
They are not chitons, or turbans
or whelks, or periwinkles —
not slugs or snails or striped-mouthed
conniwinks. They are not scallops
nor clams—neither razor nor geoduck —
nameless, they write their curious script
while we follow patiently, dictionaries
ready, our secret language.
"Do you remember the snail writing?"
we will email each other. "What
did it say?"

SUNSET AND MISERE

As the sun falls behind the small
islands of Clayoquot Sound —
saffron merging to indigo
the hills no longer a colour but a shape
upon the eye —
we play *Misery*
the first card game she taught me
that I manage to remember.
She is exasperated with me
pointing out my errors.
I am much more interested
in the dynamics between us.
"Sometimes," I joke, "I think
you were my mother in another life
and we forget our parts
this time around."
She assures me it's reciprocal
and sometimes she really is my daughter.
In this game I finally win.
She is amused. I win again.
I feel bad that she lost. "It's only a game
of luck," we agree.
Later, she beats me at Trivial Pursuits
gains a lot of mileage: "I beat my mother!"
she chortles. "And she is twice my age, and smart!"

We can barely see the cards but the wind
is so warm and our arms
still itchy from the day's heat. She snaps
the cards; a crow replies, and a whirr
in the cedars suggests an owl.
We stretch out the hours
knowing they will be tucked under pillows —
in Japan, in Victoria —
and the snap of a card, a saffron
sunset, a whirr of wings, a heartbeat
of surf will bring us
back here. This moment.

Stone of Light

If you write the iambic bongo, it goes like this
and one and two and three and four and five,
a soothing rhythm, like the waves below
that pounded all the evening, and the snow
filling the gaps of fallen branches, broken
with wind and grief. The sea is gray and sullen
mountains soft with morning light, the trees
still now, or moving slowly to a restless
beat that whispers winter. cold. and dark.
But the fire dances in the grate
its orange flames eating through the wood
as the light will eat away the darkness
and every morning will offer you a stone
of light, and the night will set it blazing.

Sundays in London
for Jeff

In London, I lived in a flat at Pont Street Mews
a block away from Harrods
where the limousines coughed out the rich
on Sunday mornings.
We'd walk over in jeans and birkenstocks —
choose strawberries arranged in red spirals, mangoes
in round pyramids, baskets of blueberries in careful symmetry.
Baguettes in long thin baskets, breads
flavoured with sage and olive and rosemary,
and cheese with names like the holidays we planned
with maps laid out on the bed: Parma, Gorgonzola, Brie.
Then we'd pick up the London Times, the weight of a dictionary,
and walk home to fresh coffee bubbling on the stove.

He took the front pages while I spread out the literary section —
the hemp carpet scratching my elbows,
his toes absently scratching my back.
Was there music? I remember only silence —
the sound of pages turning, the gulp of coffee,
the click of leaf on cobblestone
in the driveway below,
breath and bread and metallic clip of knife against plate:
the warm silence of companionship.

In those days, coffee was merely coffee:
strong or weak, with cream or sugar:
no latte, cappucino, macciatto or almond —
just the first bitter taste, the thoughtful sip
between the pages of book reviews and crosswords.
In those days, forever was something to avoid;
and plans stretched no farther than the country cottage
we'd booked for the weekend, in Cornwall.

He never grew a paunch
lost his hair
became gray and tired —
never turned his back in sleep
or sat in silence at a restaurant.
My Sunday lover, brief blossom,
sitting always in a chair by the window
while the London sun throws cool shadows
on the pages of a book
I once read and loved.

Shards

On a train to Cornwall —
the shards of a love affair
laid out in memory like the dusty table
in an archeologist's dig — jagged pieces
of words and gestures, a bright moment,
a pattern broken — to the coast,
where once Arthur sat in a stone castle
watching the sun dim
the shining armour. On her lap
a novel, a notebook, a pen. She would be
a writer, nobody would see the pieces
she had taped inside her bones —
better shards
than emptiness.

Each morning she walked
the footpaths; the sheep lifted slow
eyes as she climbed the stile, threading
carefully through the field to the cliffs
at the edge, where the sea
shook and the falcon rode
the air. In her notebook she examined
each fragment, turned her life
carefully over. Where
to go next? Pick up the patched
and shattered urn, fill it with flowers?
or let it lie with its companions
in the buried cities?

Each day the footpaths led
a little farther, to St. Isaac, St. Ives,
and her solitude cloaked her shoulders
like a summer evening. The pages
filled with air and with dust,
and the hooks of her questions
became the open palms where she held
the falcon's cry and the sound
of the shore and the long road
home.

Pivotal

4 p.m. She has entered her loneliness,
scatters her thoughts like paper
lined and unlined.

The books she has intended to read
their wings spread on the arms
of tables, the backs of couches, her bed.

Coffee and angst keep her spinning
on the axle of her body, phrases
turn in the empty air, hoping to connect something
with something.

Dips her spoon into the surface of things,
agitates the deep water. She does not know
what she knows.

The hawthorn tree outside her window —
it is the time after berries,
before blossom.

I Stop Writing

I stop writing now, when words
flop flaccid on a damp page —
fish with tired mouth
and body unknown to air.
How can I catch sky-leaping
dorado with buzz bombs
bought at the five and dime?
To reel in a big one I need
hand crafted flies, a long line in a swift river,
a slow mind full
of no matter, watching the curl
of water against a smooth rock,
the sun slide under fern and willow
drifting green fingers in the current.
I'll start writing again when the sky is sherbet,
place three rainbow trout in a dark pan,
toss their lazy bodies over a hot fire,
here, I'll say. These are all for you.

Wear and Tear

Come, he said, combing and curling
each strand of her hair between his fingers
show me your scars, your wrinkles, your signs
of wear and tear. Show me the weather
of you. You first, she said.

Here, on my hands — these heavy hills
of blue rivers, and brown puddles —
and a face, fitted badly, on a form
melting like a candle in mid summer.
Here, on my neck — lumps of no particular
belonging. And this broken bone, still
jagged along its edges, still a jolt
under skin. This scar, like a line
of ant hills — a skiing accident. And,
sliding a hand across his bald head,
this. There's still a sliver or two
of gray hair. Now your turn.

This scar, she said, like a dry river bed —
hides a titanium knee, which now
works fine. And this one, lingering
and circling, searches the cave of my belly
for a lost child. Let's not count the chin
that forgets its pride, and tucks itself
under too much skin. Let's take note
of the hair: still dark, still fine.

He tastes each scar with his tongue,
celebrates the storm, lightning with its broken
brightness, a winter rain.

A Paltry Thing

An aged man is but a paltry thing
a tattered coat upon a stick, unless
soul clap his hands and sing, and louder sing
for every tatter of its mortal dress
> W. B. Yeats, from "Sailing to Byzantium"

Shakespeare was dead by 52
Mozart and Schubert hardly past their teens
not to mention Shelley Keats and Byron
who wrote themselves out on a feather of fire.
They never had to watch their knees collapse
check their stuttering heart, weigh everything
that entered their mouth, count the raised scars —
proud flesh I've heard it called — that measure
each missing part — gall bladder, kidney, spleen:
An aged man is but a paltry thing

My niece, at two, whose skin like soft rain
encloses her without a crease or tuck
tastes of summer, smells like dew and talcum.
She jumps from table to desk to bed to floor, knees like
perfect pistons, in the morning
ready to slide into her dancing dress
her body light as chiffon.
I hold her against me, while muscles ache
feeling like, I confess,
a tattered coat upon a stick, unless

I get myself in order, do the fitness thing:
treadmill, stairmaster, aquatics, aerobics —
eat protein only or carbs only or vegetables only
six small meals or one small meal or none at all.
But no matter what we care for it,
body will not last, and that's the thing.
Might as well learn sonnets from the experts,
place words like pebbles on a forest path,
tap rhythms along a high wire of daring, let
soul clap its hands and sing, and louder sing

What else is there to do but sing?
Dance a slow tango, your partner a hooded cloak
who whirls and dips and drops you
even before the last note drifts from the cello —
What else is there to do but dance?
the grind of bone on bone, the rust of hip, the best
is past, and yet body uses groans for drums,
laments for melody; song gathers in the throat
and chants a blessing
for every tatter in its mortal dress

We Play Bridge

My mother's hands —
as she fans out the cards —
cellophane stretched from one bone
to the next, the bones
thin and gnarled. I can see her
veins, blue and pulsing, her fingernails
echoing blue. *Wait a minute,*
she says, rubbing her thumb,
plays her ace.

The skin of her face no longer fits
the high cheekbones, the stubborn chin.
It falls like drapery
around her neck.

Wistfully, she praises
my new hairstyle, short and perky.
Mine is too thin now,
she says, patting the pale strands.
Once, waves of blonde
dipped over one eye, framed
smooth cheeks.

She's deaf in one ear, hard
of hearing in the other; guesses
at my words, asks to repeat
each sentence.

At 88, she can say to me,
if I'm around then, when I tell her
my plans for the summer —
and I believe her. Yes. If.

I'm going to Copenhagen
I tell her. *What? What did you*
say you were holding? Exasperated,
I snap at her, then guilt, like a plague
of locusts — how could you?
It's not her fault. Look

at your own hands.

Coming Through

400 years in a narrow land,
our veins thick and stagnant;
blood runs thin in a place of dust.

When we crossed the Red Sea,
the waves rising like walls
and the land dry before us,
we thought we were free.

But there was the desert —
our minds could not fathom
the space, saw only sand
and no water. Sand.
No water. Our garments,
of Egyptian cotton, fell from our shoulders,
in strips and rags. The sun beat
our backs, burned our hair
white. Soon even our tears
dried in the desert air. There was rock
and no water. We sat on stone,
looking back at the green fields,
the small huts of *Mitzrayim*.
Why look forward
upon nothing?

Miriam led us from well
to well, cool water at the end
of a long day. But there was no place
to build, only a moment
of shade, sun reflected
on the palm frond, wind
scratching its spiky fingers:
wind on a hot face, a cup
of water.

Now is the time
for turning. Between us and Jericho
is only a stretch of grass,
tender green in the spring breeze,
and a wall. In my hand,
the ram's horn, a smooth bone
of sound — with my breath
I can shake the walls, stir the stones
into flight.

In front of me, the shadow of a wall,
In my hand, a trumpet.

Acknowledgements

I am grateful to the editors of the following magazines for printing some of these poems, in present or previous incarnations: *Event, Dalhousie Review, Antigonish Review, Iambs & Trochees, Wordworks,* and *Quill Literary Magazine.* Some of these poems first appeared in the chapbooks *Journey, Mythical Women, Long Beach with Lara,* and *Papa Pucky,* published by Quay Words Press.

"After Winter" was the winner of the 2003 BC Federation of Writers Literary Writes contest. "Nine Days Before Tisha B'Av" (previously titled "Shadow of Joy") was a finalist in the Mocambopo Poetry Contest 2004.

I am grateful beyond measure for the work of my editor, Susan Stenson, who shared pizza while crossing out my treasured lines, and praised profusely when there was praise to be found.

Without the support of the amazing community of writers in Victoria I would be living a lesser life. Many thanks to Wendy Morton, "fifth business" to many emerging writers. Thanks to those who have taught me about line and form and rhythm and image: Patrick Lane for his immense generosity and hard eye; Lorna Crozier, Rhona McAdam, Marlene Cookshaw, Kate Braid, Susan Stenson, Brian Brett for courses and workshops that paved the way to new poems. To Carl Leggo, who first published a poem of mine and who continues to support and encourage. But most of all, the gift of my writing group, the Wayward Ones: Yvonne Blomer, Grace Cockburn, Andrea McKenzie, Pam Porter, Karen Shklanka, Cynthia Woodman-Kerkham; the twice monthly groups have been bread and water, vitamin and ambrosia, Peace roses and southern cornbread. They feed the cells of a new life.

This book of poetry is dedicated to three people: my daughter Lara, whose photograph is the cover and the inspiration of the title; and my parents, Sol and Minnie Pelman, still going strong after 67 years together.